BASIC ✹ ESSENTIALS®
ANIMAL TRACKS

Help Us Keep This Guide Up to Date

Every effort has been made by the authors and editors to make this guide as accurate and useful as possible. However, many things can change after a guide is published—trails are rerouted, regulations change, techniques evolve, facilities come under new management, etc.

We would love to hear from you concerning your experiences with this guide and how you feel it could be improved and kept up to date. While we may not be able to respond to all comments and suggestions, we'll take them to heart and we'll also make certain to share them with the authors. Please send your comments and suggestions to the following address:

The Globe Pequot Press
Reader Response/Editorial Department
P.O. Box 480
Guilford, CT 06437

Or you may e-mail us at:

editorial@GlobePequot.com

Thanks for your input, and happy travels!

BASIC ESSENTIALS® SERIES

BASIC ✳ ESSENTIALS®

ANIMAL TRACKS

ROSEANN AND JONATHAN HANSON

The Globe Pequot Press

Guilford, Connecticut

Basic Essentials is a registered trademark of The Globe Pequot Press.

Cover photo by R. Hanson
Cover design by Lana Mullen
Text and layout design by Casey Shain and Lisa Reneson
Photo credits: pages 8, 10, 12, 16, 20, 22, 24, 26, 28, 30, 32, 34, 36, 38, 40, 42, 44, 46, 48, 52, 54, and 56 ©ArtToday; page 6, 14, 18 and 50 ©Shattil/Rozinski Photography; all other photos by Roseann and Jonathan Hanson.

Maps and illustrations by Lisa Reneson, based on original submissions from Roseann and Jonathan Hanson

Library of Congress Cataloging-in-Publication Data
Hanson, Roseann.
  Basic essentials. Animals tracks/Roseann Hanson and Jonathan Hanson.
    p. cm. — (Basic essentials series)
Includes bibliographical references (p. 69).
ISBN 0-7627-0754-2
    1. Animal tracks. I. Hanson, Jonathan. II. Title.

QL768.H36   2001
599—dc21
                                                                00-063634

Manufactured in the United States of America
First Edition/Second Printing

Contents

Introduction:
The Art of Reading Nature's Stories

Picture a grassy meadow with a small stream running across one side, tall trees and a thicket of berry bushes marking its sinuous path. It's midmorning, the sun is warm, and there are a few birds chirping, but otherwise it's perfectly still, not an animal in sight. A scene that may seem devoid of wildlife, however, remains so only to the uninitiated. If you know just a little bit about finding and reading animal footprints and evidence of their feeding and communication, you'll discover that this "empty" meadow is actually the busiest place around—a veritable Serengeti of animal activity. There are bear tracks around the berry bushes where a female black bear ate a snack; bits of crayfish shells on the stream bank and little handlike prints tell of a raccoon's breakfast; a scraped-up area the size of a dinner plate, with round pellets scattered around it, marks a cottontail's favorite dust bath; a shredded shrub is the victim of a young white-tailed buck's pre-rut jousting as he rubs the shedding velvet from his antlers; and a long set of big-cat prints walking down the meadow trail tells of a mountain lion's search for supper.

You don't have to be a grizzled old woodsman or come from a long line of Native American trackers to enjoy animal tracking or to do it well. It's not a mystical art. All you need are three well-developed skills, which we all have and can improve: observation, patience, and awareness.

Observation

Your best tool is your ability to observe a track scene and take in all the clues left by the animal—not just the physical tracks, but also details such as which way the animal was going, if the animal veered off a trail to one side or the other briefly, if it was alone or in a group, if it walked down the middle of the trail or just darted across, and if it left any other marks like scratchings or piles of scat. Each of these clues can be used to identify the animal that made the track, but you need to observe carefully as well as truthfully: It's easy to turn a track or scene into what you'd *like* it to be rather than what it is. (We have a lovely plaster cast of a large coyote track that for a week we were convinced belonged to a Mexican wolf, until we were honest about the clues and details.) Don't forget to notice physical and geographic details: habitat, topography, weather, season, and so on. Stay quiet, too—it helps concentration.

Patience

Slowing down is actually the hardest tracking skill for most people to develop. In order to practice tracking well, you need to take lots of time to observe the scene and do so slowly and methodically, from all angles (get down on your hands and knees, too). It's almost a kind of meditation. Some practitioners get into the mind or even the physical aspect of the animal: If you were a bear walking down this trail, where would you walk, what would you eat, where would you be going and when?

Awareness

Awareness of your natural surroundings is a skill that comes only with study and practice. If you are going to be a successful tracker, you need to learn about your surroundings, the plants, the animals, the weather, the seasons—what happens when, which creatures are active when, what blooms or fruits when. Learn the life histories of the animals, their eating and traveling and mating habits. This is nature awareness. It's incredibly fulfilling, and it will make you a superb tracker, because you'll know that (for example) kit foxes are almost strictly carnivores—kangaroo rats are their favorite prey—and live in the desert. You won't find them in mountain canyons, where you're more likely to find their relatives the gray foxes.

Getting Started

This book is for beginners, and it is necessarily brief—an introduction to the fun and fascination of tracking. So you'll eventually want other field guides in addition to this one: books about mammal (or bird or reptile) identification, with range maps and life history information. An advanced tracking book will be useful as well, such as Olaus J. Murie's *Animal Tracks*—a remarkable compendium of information about the natural history and tracking of North American mammals, birds, reptiles, and insects. Plant books are useful for identifying plants used by animals you are tracking. Look also for nature guides to your region.

Here are a few practical tips as you get out tracking:

- The best time to look for tracks is when the sun is at a low angle. This will cast shadows in the track depressions, making them much easier to see.

- Each animal description in this book includes tips on where to look for their tracks, but in general good spots include little-used dirt trails and back roads, water sources, and areas where there is a good food supply.

- In addition to your animal and plant ID books, you'll want to have a small ruler (preferably transparent, with both inches and centimeters; some people also carry calipers for very accurate measuring), a field notebook, and pencils and permanent ink pens. A camera is a great idea (record the picture number with the track ID and description in your notebook), as is some way of permanently capturing the track, either plaster or a tracing kit (see chapter 5).

- Practice is the only way to build on your knowledge, so get out as often as you can, and take really good notes (and bring them with you, for field reference) on every aspect of the track and your surroundings.

Use this book as a way to get started enjoying the art of tracking. Develop your three skills—observation, patience, and awareness—and build your library of notes on the tracks in your ecosystem. We provide a starting point for learning about the animals, but you'll no doubt want to delve further with other sources of natural history information. Finally, we provide information in chapter 6 on how to use animal tracking in conservation projects, so that future generations will have as much fun as we do discovering the world of animal tracking.

Identifying and Describing Animal Tracks

Key to Tracks by Size and Shape

The following key will help you identify quickly the animal tracks we discuss in this book. The first thing you need to do in identifying a track is determine its approximate size. This will tell you where to look in the key. Then judge its general shape—is it round? Oblong? Is it a hoof, or does it show toes? Use the key to identify likely animals, then turn to the pages in this book where these animals' tracks are described and illustrated.

It's important to remember that these are very general size and shape guidelines; sizes vary widely between the sexes as well as from region to region and in different substrates (the type and condition of the dirt: mud, dry dust, rocky dirt, sand, and so on). Shape can also vary depending on the substrate and even on the speed the animal was traveling when it made the track. And don't forget that there will be an occasional anomaly. For three years we tracked a female mountain lion that had an extreme extension of the third toe on both of her front feet—these toes stuck out way above the others, and so she made a very odd track, much more oblong than the usual rounded cat print.

In the following key the letter *F* refers to the front foot; *H* refers to the hind foot.

Under ½ inch (1 cm)

Round

Four Toes*	Deer mouse F (p. 15)
Five Toes*	Deer mouse H (p. 15)

1/2 inch to 1½ inches (1 to 4 cm)

Round

Four Toes*	Eastern chipmunk F (p. 17) ; Longtail weasel (p. 29); Gray fox (p. 43)
Five Toes*	Eastern chipmunk H (p.27); Striped skunk F (p. 27); Longtail weasel (p. 29); Badger H (p. 31)
Indistinct Toes	Eastern cottontail F (p. 33)
Oblong or Rectangular	Ord kangaroo rat (p. 19); Striped skunk H (p. 27)
Hoof	Javelina (p. 49)

1½ inches to 3 inches (4 to 8 cm)

Round

Four Toes*	Coyote (p. 39); Bobcat (p. 45)
Indistinct Toes	Blacktail jackrabbit F (p. 35)
Oblong or Rectangular	Woodchuck (p. 23); Porcupine (p. 25); Eastern cottontail H (p. 33); Raccoon (p. 37); Badger F (p. 31)
Hoof	White-tailed deer (p. 51)
Bird	Ruffed grouse (p. 9); Greater roadrunner (p. 11); Northern bobwhite quail (p. 7)

3 inches to 5 inches or more (8 to 12 cm)

Round

Four Toes*	Gray wolf (p. 41); Mountain lion (p. 47)
Oblong or Rectangular	Beaver (p. 21); Blacktail jackrabbit H (p. 35); Raccoon (p. 37) Black bear (p. 57)
Hoof	Elk (p. 53); Moose (p. 55)
Bird	Great blue heron (p. 13)

*Most of the time this is true, but sometimes, depending on the substrate, one digit does not print, so a print that usually has five toes may show only four.

Describing Animal Tracks

The terminology of animal tracks isn't hard, but there are a few terms you need to know:

■ *Pad:* Pads are what make the print—in most animals like cats and dogs, you see the prints from the toe pads and the plantar pad, the big pad behind the toes. In hoofed animals you see the prints left by the hoofs—either a single hoof, as in horses and similar animals, or two, as in deer, elk, and many others. In this book we don't use the technical terminology *(metatarsal, metacarpal, interdigital,* or *digital pads),* but if you'd like to learn it, see the appendix of this book for suggested reading.

■ *True track:* When you measure a track, make sure you measure the actual track and not the larger track created by the displaced soil; study the track carefully, and measure only the bottom of its plane (imagine the animal's foot making the track and pushing dirt out of the way, and measure only the part that represents the foot).

■ *Overall length and width:* Measure the total length and width of each individual track, side to side and back to front; this book, because it is for beginners, includes length only, but do record all the measurements you can.

■ *Pad length and width:* For some of the larger mammals, measurements of the larger (plantar) pads can be useful for identification.

■ *Stride:* This is the length of each step the animal makes. It can be measured from any foot: from the print of one front paw to the next print of the same paw, or a hind paw. (It doesn't matter whether you measure from the toe to the toe, or the rear of the print to the rear, as long as it's consistent.) We won't deal much with stride measurements here, but some advanced tracking books do.

■ *Straddle:* This is the distance between each foot left to

Animal Tracks **3**

right, measured from inside edge to inside edge; this book does not go into straddle measurements, which vary widely, but other books do.

- *Trail:* A track trail is simply a line of tracks from a single animal.

- *Double register:* Both carnivores and their prey sometimes walk by placing their hind feet in the same spot that they placed their front feet, thus diminishing the chance that they will make noise when stalking or hiding. Reading these tracks can be difficult, because the hind-foot track mixes with that of the front.

- *Gait:* This is the arrangement that all the tracks (front and hind, left and right) make in different modes or speeds of travel, such as walking, loping, bounding, stalking, or diagonal trotting. To understand and describe gait, you need to be able to distinguish front-foot tracks from rear-foot, an advanced tracking skill (for example, some animals' hind tracks are smaller than their front tracks). There are many good sources of information on advanced tracking techniques; see the appendix.

Getting More Specific

In the next chapter you'll find much more information about the various animals included in this book. You'll see photos of the animals, maps that show where they live, and illustrations of their tracks. Next to the tracks you'll find captions that provide specific details about the tracks.

The captions for the illustrations include average measurements of overall length of the track (both front and hind if applicable), what kind of substrate and in what habitat the sample track was taken from, and a few notes.

Animal Tracks

In this chapter we describe and illustrate a variety of tracks made by common and interesting North American mammals and birds. We have provided the following information for each animal:

Name: We have tried to list the most widely used common name for each animal, but where there's more than one, we have mentioned others in the text. We also list the scientific name, using the binomial system of genus and species; scientists occasionally change these names as they learn more about a species' genetic history.

Family: This is the scientific classification of the animal, and can be a useful clue to identification—sometimes animals in the same family leave similar tracks.

Size: The first size listed is the overall length of the animal itself. This is followed, when appropriate, by its tail length, height, and weight. These are very rough averages only—the size of individual animals varies greatly from region to region and between sexes. In general, northern animals are larger than southwestern animals, and males are bigger than females.

Habitat: Throughout North America there are many types of habitat, and we have used broad descriptions: *desert, grassland, woodland, forest,* and so on. This is the species' preferred place to live, but individuals may be found elsewhere.

Habits: Here we give you a brief life history of the animal—its behavior, feeding preferences, and any other information that can be helpful to identification.

Tracking Notes: These are tips for you on track identification, including information on similar species.

Northern Bobwhite Quail

(Colinus virginianus)

Family Odontophoridae *(New World Quail)*

Size: 9¾ inches (25 cm) long.

Habitat: Open woodlands and woodland edges, brushlands, farmlands, roadsides throughout the year.

Habits: Like most quail, northern bobwhite quail eat seeds, leaves, and insects, foraging and roosting together in small flocks, or coveys, throughout most of the year. They break up into pairs during spring and summer for breeding. They are most active in the early morning and evening.

6

Tracking Notes: There are five species of quail in the United States in addition to the bobwhite—the Montezuma quail *(Crytonyx montezumae)*, scaled quail *(Callipepla squamata)*, Gambel's quail *(Callipapla gambelii)*, California quail *(Callipepla californica)*, and mountain quail *(Oreortyx pictus)*, all of the Southwest and West. Their tracks are nearly identical. Look for quail tracks in the mud around ponds or in the soft dirt of country roads in agricultural areas. Note that quail tracks are more delicate than grouse tracks (p. 9), and often are seen in quantity.

1½ to 2 inches (3.8 to 5.1 cm)

Often in groups

Track substrate: mud

Habitat: pond edge

1½"

Northern Bobwhite Quail

Ruffed Grouse

(Bonasa umbellus)

Family Phasianidae *(Partridges, Grouse, Turkeys)*

Size: 17 inches (43 cm) long.

Habitat: Deciduous and mixed woodlands throughout the year.

Habits: In spring and summer these birds feed mainly on the ground for seeds, berries, flowers, leaves, and insects (sometimes small reptiles). In winter they feed up in trees, on buds.

Tracking Notes: There are seven species of grouse and prairie chickens in the United States—spruce grouse *(Dendragapus canadensis)* and sharp-tailed grouse *(Tympanuchus phasianellus)* of the North, blue

grouse *(D. obscurus)* and sage grouse *(Centrocercus urophasianus)* of the West, and greater and lesser prairie chickens *(Tympanuchus cupido* and *T. pallidicinctus)* of the plains. Their tracks are similar. Look for grouse tracks around dense thickets of berry bushes or, in winter, beneath deciduous trees. Grouse tracks are more robust with wider-splayed toes than quail.

2 to 2½ inches (5.1 to 6.4cm)

Track substrate: mud

Habitat: pond edge

2"

Ruffed Grouse

Greater Roadrunner

(Geococcyx californianus)

Family Cuculidae *(Cuckoos)*

Size: 23 inches (58 cm) long.

Habitat: Desert, brushlands with open country throughout the year.

Habits: Like the cartoon character, wild roadrunners do often run down or across roads, rarely flying except to glide short distances. They chase down insects, rodents, reptiles, and birds. Pairs mate for life.

Tracking Notes: The track is a distinctive elongated X, with two toes forward and two back, a pattern called *zygodactyl*. When a roadrunner is running, its tracks are about 10 to 12 inches (25 to 30 cm) apart; when walking, about 3 to 4 inches (8 to 10 cm) apart.

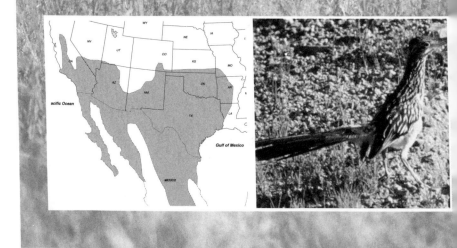

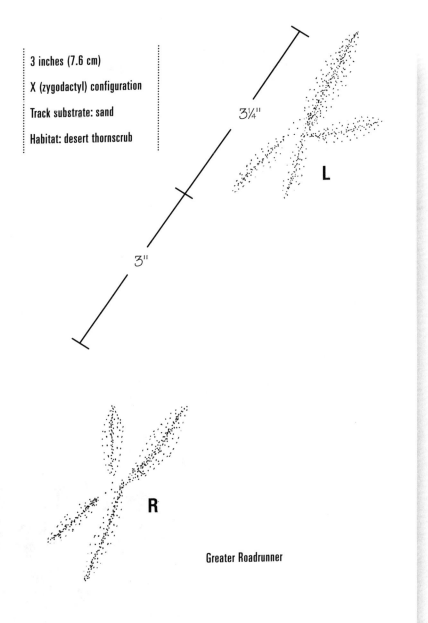

3 inches (7.6 cm)

X (zygodactyl) configuration

Track substrate: sand

Habitat: desert thornscrub

3¼"

3"

L

R

Greater Roadrunner

Great Blue Heron

(Ardea herodias)

Family Ardeidae *(Herons, Bitterns)*

Size: 46 inches (117 cm) long.

Habitat: Shores, marshes, swamps, tidal flats, ponds, creeks; year-round in central latitudes, but some move to the northern regions of the range in summer, and to southern regions in winter.

Habits: Great blue herons hunt by stalking around in shallow water, spearing fish, amphibians, and reptiles; near water, they will even eat birds and rodents.

Tracking Notes: The track trail is often nearly in a straight line. Note the asymmetrical front toes and very long rear toe, typical only of the heron family. This increases stability while standing on one leg

(as herons often do). Other heron tracks are smaller; only the great egret *(Ardea alba)* is of similar size.

6 to 8 inches (15.2 to 20.3 cm)

Asymmetrical toes

Track substrate: mud

Habitat: tidal flat

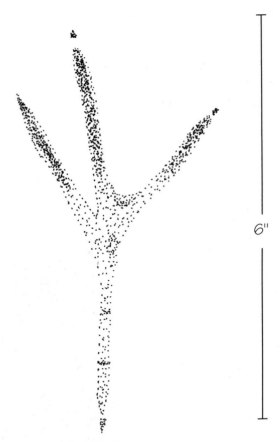

6″

Great Blue Heron

Deer Mouse

(Peromyscus maniculatus)

Family Cricetidae *(Mice, Rats, Lemmings, and Voles)*

Size: 2⅜ to 4 inches (7 to 10 cm) long, with a tail 2 to 5 inches (5 to 13 cm) long.

Habitat: Nearly all habitats: deserts, grasslands, mixed woodlands, forests, towns.

Habits: Primarily nocturnal, this omnivore (seeds, nuts, acorns, insects) is active all year. Deer mice set up house in underground burrows, holes in stumps, trees, and buildings—they are excellent climbers.

Tracking Notes: Nearly all mice leave similar footprints; depending on the substrate, the pads, toes, and claws often register as groups of dots. Note the pattern the feet make: The trail pattern, which might be called the gait, is nearly paired hind feet, with front feet slightly offset. This is typical of mice and chipmunks. Shrew tracks are similar, but generally the trail pattern of shrews is more closely spaced, and shrews tend to shuffle along. Also, mice eat seeds, leaving hulls behind, while shrews are carnivores.

¾ to ½ inch (1 to 1.3 cm)

Five toes H, four toes F

Track substrate: mud

Habitat: garden

Typical gait of a Deer Mouse

⊢— ½" —⊣

⊢— ⅜" —⊣

Deer Mouse

Eastern Chipmunk

(Tamias striatus)

Family Sciuridae *(Squirrels and Allies)*

Size: 5 to 6 inches (13 to 15 cm) long, with a tail 3 to 4 inches (8 to 10 cm) long.

Habitat: Deciduous forests, brushlands.

Habits: Chipmunks are adaptable rodents that eat seeds, fruits, bulbs, insects, and eggs; they often store their food in holes underground. They are solitary—except females with young—and defend their feeding territories. There are at least sixteen species of chipmunks in North America. Ground squirrels are similar in size and habit, but lack stripes on face.

Tracking Notes: The trail pattern is distinctive, as is the way four toes typically register on the front foot, five toes on the rear. Ground squirrel tracks are very difficult to distinguish from those of chipmunks.

½ to ¾ inch (1.3 to 1.9 cm)

Five toes H, four toes F

Track substrate: wet sand

Habitat: creekside brush

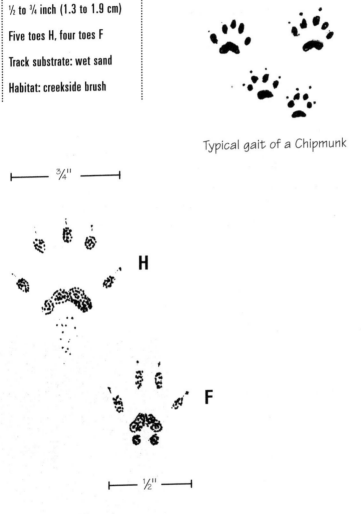

Typical gait of a Chipmunk

├── ¾" ──┤

H

F

├── ½" ──┤

Eastern Chipmunk

Ord Kangaroo Rat

(Dipodomys ordi)

Family Heteromyidae *(Pocket Mice and Kangaroo Rats)*

Size: 4 to 4½ inches (10 to 11 cm) long, with a tail 5 to 6 inches (13 to 15 cm) long.

Habitat: Deserts and desert grasslands.

Habits: Kangaroo rats, nocturnal residents of arid and semi-arid lands in the western United States, are so well adapted to dry conditions that they can get all their water needs from their food. They are so named because they have large, powerful hind legs on which they hop at high speeds or stand upright to forage, and despite the name they are mice, not rats. Kangaroo rats gather seeds and store them in chambers in extensive underground burrows, which may have many access

Gulf
of
Mexico

18

holes and are topped by large mounds of earth up to 3 feet (1 m) high and 10 feet (3 m) wide. There are at least twelve species.

Tracking Notes: Kangaroo rat tracks are distinctive— when an animal is foraging slowly, the long, triangular hind-foot heel shows clearly, as does the dragging of the long tail. When it's hopping quickly, tracks may not register clearly. Some species have four hind toes, some have five. The front feet rarely register clearly. Little mounds and depressions in the dirt indicate digging for buried seeds. Look for these tracks on sandy roads in arid lands (look to the sides of the road), or around their burrows; shallow depressions near holes may be dust "bathtubs."

Digging

Mounds

Ord Kangaroo Rat

1"

5/8"

3½"

1 to 2 inches (2.5 to 5.1 cm) H

3 to 4 inches (7.6 to 10.2 cm)
Tail drag common

Track substrate: dust

Habitat: arid grassland

Beaver
(Castor canadensis)

Family Castoridae *(Beavers)*

Size: 25 to 30 inches (64 to 76 cm) long, with a tail about 9 to 10 inches (23 to 25 cm) long; 40 to 60 pounds (18 to 27 kg).

Habitat: Streams, lakes, ponds with trees on or near banks.

Habits: This largest of our North American rodents is nocturnal in much of its wide range, preferring to gnaw at night on the bark and small twigs of trees such as alder, aspen, poplar, birch, maple, willow, and cottonwood. Pairs and family members build dams across streams to create deep, slow water under which to build their living quarters, or lodges. Some populations build dens in banksides instead.

Tracking Notes: Look for the distinctive web-footed hind-foot tracks of beavers in the mud near their dams and lodges, though perfect tracks are hard to find, since the heavy paddle-shaped tail drags over the tracks. River otter tracks are smaller, usually show in two-by-two bounding hops, and often do not indicate the hind-foot web. Other beaver sign includes cut (felled) trees and peeled logs and twigs, with tooth marks from ⅛ to ¼ inch (32 to 64 mm) wide, and scent "signposts," mud or mud-and-debris piles on which the beaver leaves territory-marking scent from special glands.

Typical trail

6 to 6½ inches (15.2 to 16.5 cm) H

Track substrate: mud

Habitat: river

6½"

F

H

Beaver

Woodchuck

(Marmota monax)

Family Sciuridae *(Squirrels and Allies)*

Size: 16 to 20 inches (41 to 51 cm) long, with a tail 4 to 7 inches (10 to 18 cm) long; 15 to 20 pounds (7 to 9 kg).

Habitat: Woodlands (especially rocky and brushy areas), ravines.

Habits: Large squirrels common in the woodlands of the eastern United States and much of Canada, woodchucks eat mostly succulent plant material. They forage during the day around their burrows, which are usually located in open meadows or meadow edges, especially near rocks or logs. Woodchucks hibernate in winter.

Tracking Notes: The closely related yellowbelly marmot *(Marmota flaviventris)* lives in the western United States, mostly in the Rocky Mountains, Cascades, and Sierra Nevadas, while the hoary marmot *(M. caligata)* lives in Alaska, British Columbia, Washington, and Idaho.

Woodchuck and marmot tracks are nearly identical. Typically, four toes register of the front foot and five of the hind foot, much like the tracks of their squirrel and chipmunk relatives. Sometimes the rear heel does not imprint, causing the rear track to appear smaller than the front one. When an animal is walking, the hind foot often double registers in the front-foot track; when it's running, the track trail is similar to that of chipmunks and squirrels. Raccoon tracks can appear similar, but the front-foot track of a raccoon shows five toes.

1½ to 2 inches (3.8 to 5.1 cm) F

2 to 2¼ inches (5.1 to 5.7 cm) H

Track substrate: dry dirt

Habitat: woodland, rocky ravine

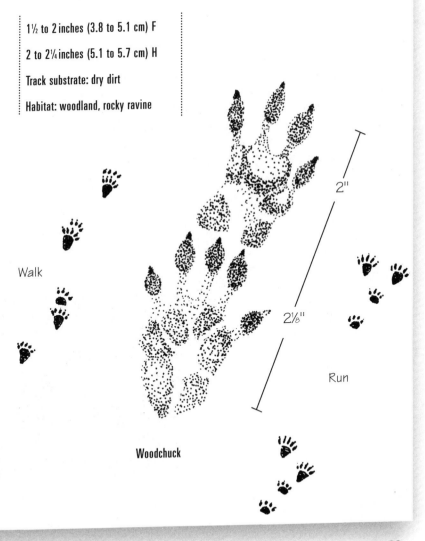

Walk

2"

2⅛"

Run

Woodchuck

Porcupine

(Erethizon dorsatum)

Family Erethizontidae *(Porcupines)*

Size: 18 to 22 inches (46 to 56 cm) long, with a tail 7 to 9 inches (18 to 23 cm) long; 10 to 25 pounds (5 to 11 kg).

Habitat: Woodlands and forests, occasionally shrublands.

Habits: Porcupines are heavy and clumsy, and prefer to climb, however awkwardly, in the relative safety of trees as they munch buds, twigs, and inner bark. Most often nocturnal, porcupines are also solitary, although there have been reports that they form small social groups in winter. During the day they sleep in hollow logs or dens and rock crevices. They mate in fall, when the usually quiet males grunt, groan, and broadcast high-pitched calls.

Tracking Notes: Porcupine feet are unique, with large, callused pads; the waddling gait shows as toed-in tracks, but the dragging tail and spines often obscure much of the track trail; as if someone walked along dragging a broom. Look in and below trees for gnawed branches, bark, and twigs.

2⅜ to 2 inches (6.0 cm) H

Track substrate: damp dirt (back road)

Habitat: woodland

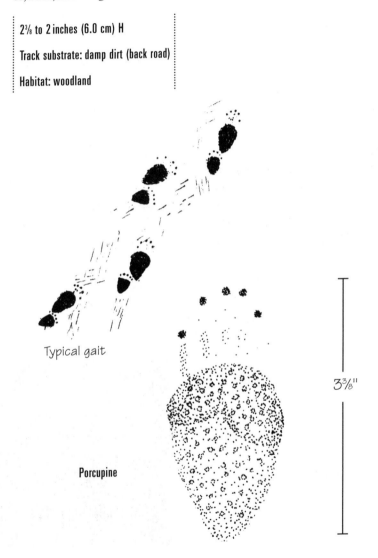

Typical gait

Porcupine

3⅜"

Striped Skunk

(Mephitis mephitis)

Family Mustelidae *(Skunks and Allies)*

Size: 13 to 18 inches (33 to 46 cm) long, with a tail 7 to 10 inches (18 to 25 cm) long; 6 to 14 pounds (3 to 6 kg).

Habitat: Mixed woodlands and semi-open country.

Habits: There are four species of skunks in North America, and all of them are voracious omnivores—they'll eat anything from meat to seeds to grubs to carrion—and although they prefer nocturnal activity, they will forage during the daytime. The striped skunk is the most widespread and commonly seen species. Although usually solitary, females will den together in winter (they do not hibernate). Natural densities are one skunk per 10 acres (4 ha), but numbers are much higher around campgrounds and suburban or cabin communities.

BASIC ESSENTIALS

Tracking Notes: The striped skunk is the most widespread of the four species and has nearly the largest tracks; the spotted skunk *(Spilogale putorius)* is also widespread but is diminutive, only 9 to 13 inches (23 to 33 cm) long; the hognose skunk *(Conepatus leuconotus)* is slightly larger than the striped, but like the slightly smaller hooded skunk *(Mephitis macroura)*, it is a southwestern species. The smaller track of the spotted skunk is easy to distinguish from the others by its small size, the frequent lack of a heel depression, and its darting, active track trail. Striped skunks move more deliberately and, being heavier, more often leave a full heel track.

1 to 1½ inches (2.5 to 3.8 cm) F

1½ to 1⅞ inches (3.8 to 4.8 cm) H

Track substrate: moist dirt (creekside trail)

Habitat: woodland

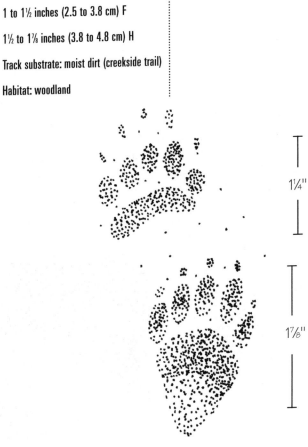

1¼"

1⅞"

Striped Skunk

Longtail Weasel

Mustela frenata

Family Mustelidae (*Skunks and Allies*)

Size: 8 to 10½ inches (20 to 27 cm) long, with a tail about 3 to 6 inches (8 to 15 cm) long; 3 to 12 ounces (85 to 340 g).

Habitat: Nearly all habitats with access to water.

Habits: Although widespread, the secretive weasel is rarely seen because its preferred time to hunt is at night. Small but fierce, longtail weasels eat rodents and even rabbits, as well as birds and reptiles. Most often they hunt along the water's edge—creeks, ponds, lakes. They are solitary, and seek shelter and make their nests in burrows dug by other animals. Like all their relatives in the mustelid family, they have very aromatic scent glands. In winter most longtail weasels molt their brown pelts into white, which is valuable to trappers (southwestern weasels are not known to have white winter coats).

Tracking Notes: The least weasel *(Mustela rixosa)* and the shorttail weasel *(M. erminea)* live mostly in the northern United States and Canada, with the shorttail's range extending south into California, Nevada, Utah, and Colorado. Look for weasel tracks—and the tracks of the related marten *(Martes americana),* mink *(Mustela vison),* and fisher *(Martes pennanti)*—along creeks and the edges of ponds, where the animals like to hunt. They leave rounded tracks like cats, but the main pad often does not print completely, nor do all five toes (four is more common). In snow, weasel tracks are characteristically twinned, indicating a bounding gait. Except for the tracks of the fisher, which are 2 to 2¼ inches (5 to 6 cm) long, the tracks of the other weasels and their kin are very difficult to distinguish.

1 to 1½ inches (2.5 to 3.8 cm) F

1½ to 1¾ inches (3.8 to 4.4 cm) H

Track substrate: moist dirt (creekside trail)

Habitat: woodland

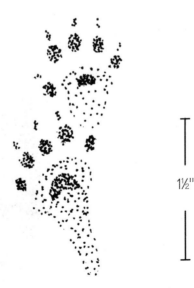

1½"

Longtail Weasel

Badger

(Taxidea taxus)

Family Mustelidae *(Skunks and Allies)*

Size: 18 to 22 inches (46 to 56 cm) long, with a tail 4 to 6 inches (10 to 15 cm) long; 13 to 25 pounds (6 to 11 kg).

Habitat: Deserts and grasslands.

Habits: Badgers are surprisingly fierce for their squat, wide-bodied size; one was known to attack the tire of a truck that it felt was violating its territory. They hunt rodents by digging furiously with long, hooked claws until their prey is uncovered and caught. Although mostly active at night, they will venture out in cool mornings or late afternoons. Naturalists have observed coyotes and badgers cooperating on a hunt, or at least taking advantage of each other: While a badger digs for a rodent, the coyote sits at one of the rodent's other escape holes to snatch it up when it runs out—but sometimes the presence of the

coyote causes the rodent to hold tight, allowing the badger to grab it. Badgers dig their own large burrows in embankments or slopes, usually shaded by a shrub or tree.

Tracking Notes: Badger tracks are distinctly toed-in, and at least some of the long claws usually show. Sign of badger foraging includes lots of energetically dug holes, often with big rocks pulled out; like their relatives the skunks, they tend to dig along favorite paths or roadside berms. Badger den holes are shaped like badgers: wider than they are tall, about 8 inches (20 cm) high and 12 inches (25 cm) wide.

1¾ to 2 inches (4.4 to 5.1 cm) F

1¼ to 1½ inches (3.2 to 3.8 cm) H

Tracks toed-in; front feet are larger

Track substrate: moist dirt (roadside puddle edge)

Habitat: dessert grassland

1 ¾"

Badger

Eastern Cottontail

(Sylvilagus floridanus)

Family Leporidae *(Hares and Rabbits)*

Size: 14 to 17 inches (35 to 43 cm) long; 2 to 4 pounds (1 to 2 kg).

Habitat: Brushy and weedy areas, meadow and forest edges.

Habits: The common "bunny rabbits" in most of the Midwest and East, as well as northern Mexico, eastern cottontails are active mostly from the early evening until the late morning. During the warmer parts of the day, they rest in little depressions in the dirt called *forms,* in their burrows, or in the deep shade of dense shrubs or brush piles. In spring and summer cottontails eat grasses or forbs; in winter, twigs and bark.

Tracking Notes: There are four other species of closely related (and difficult to differentiate) cottontails in the United States and Mexico: desert *(Sylrilagus auduboni),* mountain *(S. nuttalli),* New England *(S.*

transitionalis), and brush *(S. bachmani).* The swamp *(S. aquaticus)* and marsh rabbits *(S. palustris)* are unique in their wetland habitats. The four cottontails leave nearly identical tracks, usually without distinct pads and toe markings—two elongated rear feet and two round front feet, often with the rear feet placed before the front; swamp and marsh rabbits leave more distinct toe and pad marks. Cottontails leave conspicuous rabbit-sized dust-bath depressions, with scratch marks and sometimes droppings, near their burrows and favorite foraging areas (p. 61). Jackrabbit tracks are larger—2½ inches (6 cm) and up to 5 inches (13 cm, in snow) for hind feet—and the distance between track groups is greater.

2 to 3½ inches (5.1 to 8.9 cm) H

1 to 1⅜ inches (2.5 to 3.5 cm) F

Track size varies, especially hind feet

Track substrate: dust (back road)

Habitat: woodland

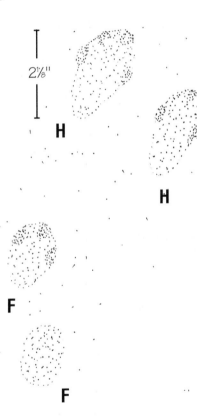

2⅞"

H

H

F

F

Eastern Cottontail

Blacktail Jackrabbit

(Lepus californicus)

Family Leporidae *(Hares and Rabbits)*

Size: 17 to 21 inches long (43 to 53 cm); 3 to 7 pounds (1 to 3 kg).

Habitat: Grasslands and deserts.

Habits: Like its little relative the cottontail, the blacktail jackrabbit is active from the early evening through the morning, retiring a little earlier than the cottontail. Blacktails browse on forbs and grasses and rest in dense shade during the day; they do not have dens. Jackrabbits are tall and often move with a loping walk rather than hopping, though they do hop—sometimes as far as 10 feet (3.3 m) per hop when traveling fast, which they do, up to 35 mph (56 km/h).

Tracking Notes: The track pattern is highly variable because when they're walking, blacktails leave tracks that can look similar to coyote, and when they're hopping quickly, the track sets can be very far apart and thus hard to follow. To help you distinguish, look for the classic rabbit pattern of paired hind feet placed in front of the front feet. Dirt roads in deserts and grasslands are good places to find jackrabbit tracks. Tracks of the whitetail jackrabbit *(Lepus townsendi)* of the plains, the antelope jackrabbit *(L. alleni)* of the Southwest and Mexico, and the European hare *(L. europaeus)* introduced in the East are nearly identical to those of the blacktail; the range and habitat of the animals can help you distinguish species.

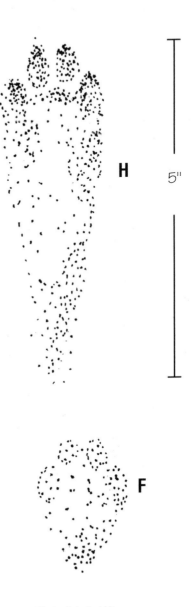

4 to 6 inches (10.2 to 15.2 cm) H

1½ to 2 inches (3.8 to 5.1 cm) F

Track size varies, especially hind feet; hops or walks

Track substrate: sand

Habitat: desert

Blacktail Jackrabbit

Raccoon

(Procyon lotor)

Family Procyonidae *(Raccoons and Allies)*

Size: 18 to 28 inches (46 to 71 cm) long, with a tail 8 to 12 inches (20 to 30 cm) long; 12 to 35 pounds (5 to 15 kg).

Habitat: Near wetlands, waterways, bodies of water, and oceans, especially with adjacent woodlands or rocky outcrops.

Habits: The ubiquitous masked raccoon well deserves its reputation as a clever troublemaker. Raccoons are omnivorous—they eat anything from fruit and nuts to invertebrates, frogs, and fish, to garbage and dog food in suburban areas—and they have powerful and dexterous front paws with which they crack open crayfish or pry open garbage cans and climb trees or porch posts. They use dens in rock crevices, underground holes, or tree or log hollows to raise their young or spend cold periods in winter, although they do not hibernate.

Tracking Notes: Raccoons leave distinctive tracks when their toes print: The front foot looks like a miniature human hand, with five long fingers; the hind foot is similar to the human foot, with five long toes, but the heel and foot pad is diamond shaped and elongated. Look for raccoon tracks in mud alongside creeks, lakes, or the ocean; their foraging will be evident in discarded bits of animal carcasses. Raccoons have two relatives in North America, the coati *(Nasua narica)* and the ringtail *(Bassariscus astutus).* Coatis live in mountain canyons of Mexico, southern Arizona, and New Mexico, and often travel in large troops; their tracks are similar to those of raccoons but lack the elongated toes. Ringtails are more solitary, live in chaparral and canyon country, are very small—2 pounds (1 kg)—and leave tiny, catlike tracks.

2 to 4 inches (5.1 to 10.2 cm) H

Bulbous toes show looks, like human hand, hind is larger

Track substrate: mud

Habitat: mountain canyon (Southwest)

Typical gait

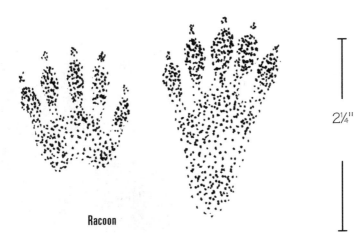

Racoon

2¼"

Coyote

(Canis latrans)

Family Canidae *(Dogs, Wolves, and Allies)*

Size: 32 to 37 inches (81 to 94 cm) long, with a tail 11 to 16 inches (28 to 40 cm) long; 20 to 50 pounds (9 to 22 kg).

Habitat: Most habitats in North America.

Habits: One of the emblematic animals of the American West, the coyote actually lives from Alaska south into Mexico, and is expanding into eastern and northeastern states. Coyotes are not uncommon in most cities within their range. One reason they are so successful is that they eat anything from plant matter to carrion, and everything in between; they will kill deer and sheep and calves, usually working in a team or pack. Housecats are a favorite prey in urban areas. Although largely nocturnal, they are active whenever prey is active, and for coyotes that's anytime. They dig dens into embankments, well hidden by brush.

Tracking Notes: Coyotes will cruise up to 10 miles (16 km) or so on a foraging expedition, and they will often take the easiest route, such as a dirt road or trail—look for their small, delicate tracks (like a flower) trotting straight down the middle. You can also look for the telltale "diagonal trot" common to wild dogs (although they do not always make this pattern): wild and some domestic dogs will trot with their body at a diagonal aspect to their line of travel, so that the tracks of the front feet land on one side of the track trail, while those of the hind feet land on the other (see illustration). Claws don't always show. Like many mammals, coyotes increase in size (and likewise their tracks are larger) in northern latitudes. Domestic dog tracks are "messier" (the toes often splay much more than a coyote's), and they do not tend to trot purposefully down the middle of trails; instead they wander hither and yon. Fox tracks are smaller and barely leave pad and toe marks. Wolf tracks are much larger, and robust.

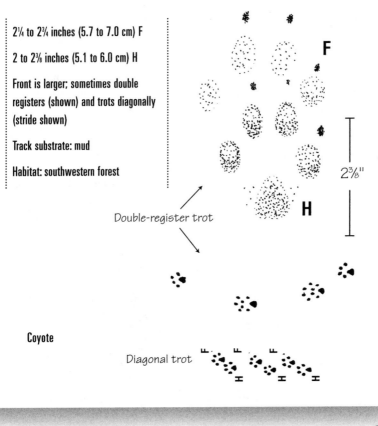

2¼ to 2¾ inches (5.7 to 7.0 cm) F

2 to 2⅜ inches (5.1 to 6.0 cm) H

Front is larger; sometimes double registers (shown) and trots diagonally (stride shown)

Track substrate: mud

Habitat: southwestern forest

F

2⅜"

H

Double-register trot

Coyote

Diagonal trot

Gray Wolf

(Canis lupus)

Family Canidae *(Dogs, Wolves, and Allies)*

Size: 43 to 48 inches (109 to 122 cm) long, with a tail 12 to 20 inches (66 to 72 cm) long; 70 to 120 pounds (31 to 54 kg).

Habitat: Forests and tundra.

Habits: The gray wolf, also called the timber wolf, is one of the last great—but now rare—predators of North America, its haunting howl an icon of wilderness. Forming packs of up to twelve or more individuals during the nonbreeding season, wolves hunt big game, such as caribou and deer, as well as elk, sheep, and small cattle. They also eat rodents and other small mammals and birds, and are not known to attack people. Like coyotes, they are active whenever their prey is moving around, night or day, and they cover great distances when hunting, often using favorite trails. Wolves dig dens in embankments or rocky outcrops, where they are protected but also able to see danger approaching.

Gray wolf has been reintroduced in these areas.

Tracking Notes: Wolf tracks, like those of their relatives the coyotes and foxes, are distinctly rectangular—longer than they are wide (rather than quite round, like cats' tracks). Look for the diagonal trot (see Tracking Notes for the coyote, p. 39), and look for tracks along trails in areas where wolves are known to hunt. Claws show more often than in coyotes. Wolf dens are much larger than coyote dens. In Arizona, New Mexico, and northern Mexico, the Mexican wolf *(Canis lupus baileyi)* was once a much more common predator, but by the middle of the 20th century the species was all but extinct. By the beginning of 2000 several packs had been reintroduced in the Blue Range Wilderness of Arizona, on the New Mexico border, and some Mexican biologists think a few wild wolves might survive in their country. Mexican wolves are slightly smaller bodied than gray wolves of the North.

4¼ to 4¾ inches (10.9 to 12.1 cm) F

3¾ to 4½ inches (9.5 to 11.4 cm) H

Front is larger; same gaits as other canines; toes splay more than coyote

Track substrate: mud

Habitat: forest

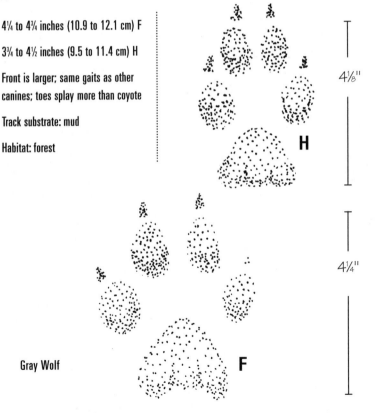

H

4⅛"

F

4¼"

Gray Wolf

Gray Fox

(Urocyon cinereoargenteus)

Family Canidae *(Dogs, Wolves, and Allies)*

Size: 21 to 29 inches (53 to 74 cm) long, with a tail 11 to 16 inches (28 to 41 cm) long; 7 to 13 pounds (3 to 6 kg).

Habitat: Oak and deciduous woodlands, mountain canyons, chaparral, and high desert.

Habits: The gray fox is a very unusual canine, for it has semiretractable claws and readily climbs trees to eat bird eggs and nestlings. Gray foxes also eat small mammals, insects, fruits, and nuts. Nocturnal hunters, gray foxes are very secretive and thus rarely seen, except perhaps darting across backcountry roads. They den in hollow logs or in holes in rocky outcrops or embankments.

Tracking Notes: The gray fox is smaller than its bushy coat and tail advertise; weighing about as much as a housecat, they barely leave discernible tracks except in mud. Their rear-foot tracks often lack the complete main pad—just a small oval, the center. Claws rarely show. Look for their tracks along roads or around canyon creeks. The even smaller kit or swift foxes *(Vulpes velox)* of the western United States and northern Mexico leave similar tracks to those of the gray fox, but usually (not always) slightly smaller, and usually in more arid and open-country habitats. The red fox *(V. vulpes)* is widespread in North America; its tracks are usually distinct from those of other foxes in that its feet are furred on the bottom, making fuzzy tracks, and if the main pad prints it usually shows a distinctive raised horizontal ridge (like a bar) across the pad.

1¼ to 2 inches (3.2 to 5.1 cm) F

1 to 1½ inches (2.5 to 3.8 cm) H

Front is larger; some gaits as other canines; rear pad often barely registers

Track substrate: dust

Habitat: desert grassland/canyon mouth

H

Double-register
track set shown

1⅛"

F

Gray Fox

Bobcat

(Felis rufus)

Family Felidae *(Cats and Allies)*

Size: 25 to 30 inches (63 to 76 cm) long, with a 5-inch (12 cm) tail; 15 to 35 pounds (6 to 16 kg).

Habitat: Forests, woodlands, canyonlands, deserts.

Habits: Bobcats are very adaptable and have become increasingly common in suburban areas within their habitats. Although primarily nocturnal, they will hunt in the early morning or late afternoon for preferred prey such as rabbits and birds (especially in suburban areas, where bird feeders provide convenient snack bars). They make their dens in hollows of logs or under rocks.

Tracking Notes: Bobcats prefer the cover of thickets and woodlands rather than open trails, so when they travel—which they do for 25 to 50 miles (40 to 80 km) within their hunting range—they do not often leave noticeable track sets like the wild dogs that trot for great dis-

tances down trails or roads. Look for bobcat tracks crossing roads or trails, but rarely walking down them for appreciable distances. Although superficially similar in size to their canine counterparts (bobcat/coyote; mountain lion/wolf), feline tracks are rounder in overall shape than canine, with proportionally more main pad showing (more often showing a three-lobed base of the main pad) and rounder toe pads (oval in dogs). Mustelid tracks usually show five toes, cats (and dogs) four. Bobcat tracks are smaller than mountain lion tracks, although a large male bobcat's track might be close to that of a young lion, especially female. Lynx *(Lynx canadensis)* tracks show fur between the wide-spread toes, obscuring the pads.

1½ to 1¾ inches (3.8 to 4.4 cm) H

1¾ to 2 inches (4.4 to 5.1 cm) F

Front is larger; note roundness of toes and overall track

Track substrate: dust

Habitat: mountain canyon

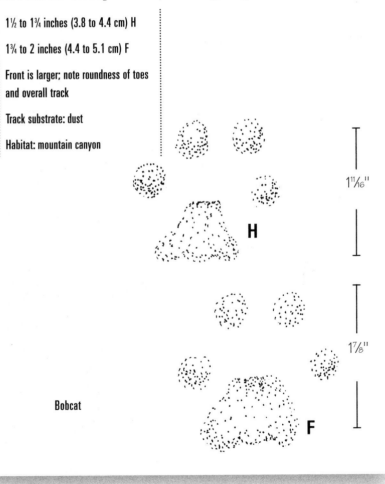

H

F

1¹¹⁄₁₆"

1⅞"

Bobcat

Mountain Lion

(Felis concolor)

Family Felidae *(Cats and Allies)*

Size: 42 to 54 inches (107 to 137 cm) long, with a tail 30 to 36 inches (76 to 91 cm) long; 80 to 200 pounds (36 to 90 kg).

Habitat: Mountain forests and woodlands.

Habits: Rarely seen, mountain lions nonetheless thrive in most of the mountains of the American West, western Canada, and Mexico. Also called pumas and cougars, they are expanding into the eastern United States. Their ranges are closely tied to the presence of plentiful deer, mostly the whitetail, but they do eat smaller mammals, cattle, and sheep. Where humans have encroached on their habitat and diminished their prey, instances of humans attacked by lions have increased. Lions' home ranges are large—100 square miles (259 square km) or so for males, less for females—and they move widely in these ranges; 20 miles (32 km) a night is not uncommon.

Tracking Notes: See Tracking Notes for the bobcat (p.44–45) for information on distinguishing feline and canine tracks. Unlike their smaller relative the bobcat, lions will walk for long distances down back roads and trails. When stalking, they will (like other predators) double register (see chapter 2), but when they walk at cruising speed, all four feet will register separately. Lions use their feet to make scrapes (p. 61)—piles of dirt or leaves on which they urinate or defecate as scent markers, or "signposts," for delineating territory or communicating mating availability to other lions. After they make a kill, lions drag their prey to thick cover and may eat just a portion of it (often the main organs) before partially burying the rest, returning several days in a row until it is gone (p. 62). In lion country look for their tracks and scrapes on back roads and trails (scrapes will be beside trails), and keep your eye out for drag marks of prey.

3 to 3¾ inches (7.6 to 9.5 cm) F

Track substrate: dry dirt (back road)

2¾ to 3 inches (7.0 to 7.6 cm) H

Habitat: mountain canyon

Front is larger; note roundness of toes, overall track; male track shown

3⅝"

Mountain Lion

F

Javelina

(Tayassu tajacu)

Family Tayassuidae *(Peccaries)*

Size: 34 to 36 inches (86 to 91 cm) long; 40 to 50 pounds (18 to 23 kg).

Habitat: Deserts and semidesert shrublands.

Habits: Called javelina (haav-a-LEE-na) or peccaries, these common wild "pigs" of the Southwest and Mexico patrol their territories in groups of several to perhaps twenty-five if food is plentiful. From the late afternoon through the early morning, they forage for seeds, fruits, cactus pads, grubs, bird eggs, and invertebrates. They breed throughout the year, and so you might see little rust-colored spotted young (called *reds*) anytime, but be careful: Javelina are fiercely protective of their herd, and have long, sharp canines.

Tracking Notes: Javelina tracks can be distinguished from deer by their blunt tips—the track looks like two human thumbprints pressed side by side into the dirt. Look for them around water holes, near creeks, and, in suburban areas, around bird feeders.

1¼ to 1½ inches (3.2 to 3.8 cm) F

1 to 1⅜ inches (2.5 to 3.5 cm) H

Front is larger; often in herds

Track substrate: dry dirt

Habitat: upland desert

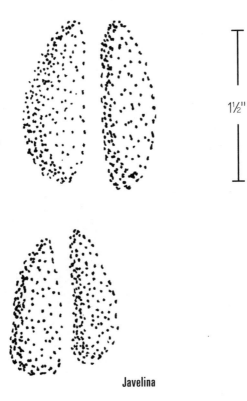

1½"

1⅜"

Javelina

White-Tail Deer

(Odocoileus virginianus)

Family Cervidae *(Deer and Allies)*

Size: 3 to 3½ feet tall (91 to 107 cm); males, 75 to 400 pounds (34 to 180 kg); females, 50 to 250 pounds (23 to 113 kg).

Habitat: Forests and woodlands.

Habits: The most widespread deer in North America, the whitetail is best known for its wide, short tail with a white underside, which it holds up like a flag when alarmed (hence its other name, flagtail). Whitetails browse forbs and new grasses, leaves, twigs, fungi, and acorns. In fall and winter bucks gather up large herds, or "harems," of females in preparation for the rut, or breeding season, using their antlers to fight each other for dominance. In summer females stay in groups of two or three, usually mothers and last year's offspring or young-of-the-year.

Tracking Notes: The Coues' whitetail *(Odocoileus virginianus cousei)*, an acknowledged subspecies found in the Southwest and Mexico, is the smallest form of whitetail. Distinguishing whitetail tracks from those of the mule deer *(O. hemionus)*, a western desert and grassland species, is difficult if not impossible because their sizes overlap, but habitat can provide a clue (although when they occur in the same area, they can mix at woodland-grassland edges). So can one trait: When running, whitetails gallop like horses and rabbits, planting their powerful hind feet far ahead of their front feet; mule deer bound or "pogo," with all four feet striking the ground at once, an action called *stotting* or *pronking.* In late summer and fall males' antlers have regrown (they drop off in spring), and they scrape off the velvet covering by thrashing their antlers in trees; look for twisted, damaged, tangled shrubs.

2¾ to 3 inches (7.0 to 7.6 cm) F or H, eastern

1¾ to 2 inches (4.4 to 5.1 cm) F or H, southwestern (Coues')

Track substrate: dry dirt

Habitat: woodland

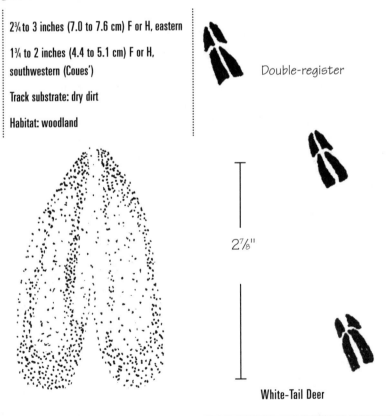

Double-register

2⅞"

White-Tail Deer

Elk

(Cervus canadensis)

Family Cervidae *(Deer and Allies)*

Size: 4 to 5 feet (122 to 152 cm) tall; males, 700 to 1,000 pounds (315 to 450 kg); females, 500 to 600 pounds (225 to 270 kg).

Habitat: Semi-open forests and woodlands, meadows.

Habits: Also called wapiti, elk are majestic forest dwellers, foraging together in large breeding herds in winter—by breeding season the bulls have formed "harems" of females—and in summer, in small single-sex groups, usually females and young and old or young males together. During breeding season, the "rut," males do battle and bugle loudly as they vie for females. Elk browse huge quantities of forbs, grasses, twigs, and bark in the morning and early evening, and at night if the moon is bright. During winter they migrate down into the lower woodlands; in spring they head back to the high country.

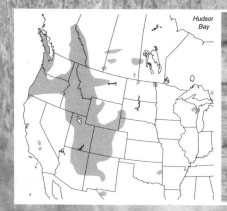

BASIC ESSENTIALS

Tracking Notes: Elk tracks are much larger and rounder than deer tracks, but can be hard to distinguish from young cattle, with which they often share habitat; look around for adult cow tracks and droppings (although even elk pellets and young cow "pies" can be similar if they are eating similar foods). Moose tracks are usually longer, sharper, and more elongated than elk tracks, but they can also be very hard to tell for sure. In late summer male elk shed the velvet on their new racks and, like their relatives the deer, will rub them in shrubs and trees to help the process; look for thrashed, tangled, broken shrubs or small trees. In fall during the rut, bulls will wallow in mud puddles and ponds; sometimes they use the same ones each year. Elk (and moose) love to eat aspen bark, so look at elk-head-level for spots of stripped-off bark, and old black scars from years of gnawing.

3⅞ to 4¾ (9.8 to 12.1 cm) F or H

Track substrate: dried mud

Habitat: southwestern forest

3⅞"

Elk

Moose

(Alces alces)

Family Cervidae *(Deer and Allies)*

Size: 5 to 6 ½ feet (152 to 198 cm) tall; males, 850 to 1,180 pounds (382 to 531 kg); females, 600 to 800 pounds (270 to 360 kg).

Habitat: Forests, near bodies of water.

Habits: The ungainly-looking moose is actually a pretty fierce protector of its young and can move surprisingly fast if it wants to. Otherwise, moose spend most of their time browsing leisurely on aquatic vegetation—they don't hesitate to enter and stay in water for long periods—supplemented by forbs, twigs, bark, and saplings, especially willow but also aspen and other forest trees. Moose are strong swimmers, having been clocked at speeds up to 35 mph (56 km/h). They are solitary, and unlike their relatives the deer and elk, bulls do not form "harems" during the fall rut.

Tracking Notes: See Tracking Notes for elk (p. 53) for differentiating from moose. Moose foraging sign includes willows and saplings of other trees such as cottonwoods broken over at the tops, with the leaves stripped from the bent-over twigs, as well as trees such as fir and aspen being stripped of all low (as high up as a moose can reach) branches and twigs—as if a meticulous groundskeeper has been at work.

4¼ to 5¼ inches (10.9 to 13.3 cm) F or H

Track substrate: mud

Habitat: forest wetland

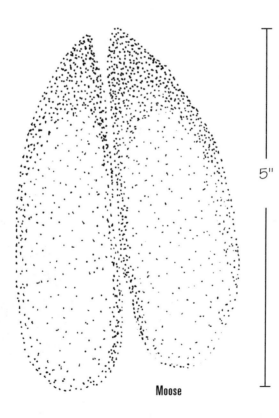

5"

Moose

Black Bear

(Ursus americanus)

Family Ursidae *(Bears)*

Size: 5 to 6 feet (152 to 183 cm) long, 2 to 3 feet (61 to 91 cm) tall at shoulders; 200 to over 475 pounds (90 to over 214 kg).

Habitat: Forests and woodlands.

Habits: Although one of our largest carnivores, the black bear actually eats mostly tubers, berries, nuts, and insects and their larvae, rounded out with deer, small mammals, eggs, carrion, and (unfortunately) garbage and pet food in suburban areas. It is in these areas where humans have encroached on bear habitat that bears have attacked people. Black bears are active mostly at night during spring and summer; in winter in most areas, they will hibernate in dens.

Tracking Notes: Bears follow favorite feeding routes in their territories and do use the easiest thoroughfares, so look for their tracks along trails and roads; during summer look around fruiting shrubs especially,

and look for torn-up old logs and turned-over rocks (where they have searched for insects). On bear feet the "big toe" is actually the outside toe (equivalent of the human pinkie toe). The round heel pad of the front foot often does not register, and in soft dirt the small inside toe (equivalent to the human big toe) often will not print, leaving a four-toed print. Bears also use trees: They bite off strips of bark to get at the sweet sap and will also rub against a favorite, sometimes biting and clawing it repeatedly, leaving it scarred. Grizzly bears (*Ursus arctos horribilis*) live in the northern United States, up into Canada and Alaska, in forest and tundra habitat. They are much larger than black bears—6 to 7 feet (183 to 213 cm) long and 325 to 850 pounds (147 to 386 kg)—and will kill mammals as large as elk. However, they more often dig for rodents—marmots are a favorite—with their huge claws, and consume a great deal of fruit, grasses, insects, and fish. To tell grizzly tracks from those of black bears, draw a straight line from the bottom of the big toe across the top of the metatarsal pad of the front-foot track. If the line intersects the little toe in the middle or above, it is a black bear; if it intersects in the bottom half or not at all, it is a grizzly.

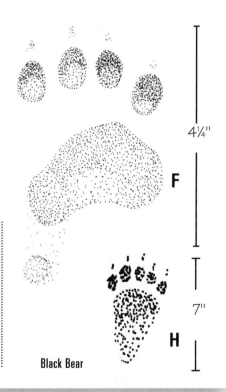

4¼"

F

4 to 4½ inches (10.2 to 11.4 cm) F

7 to 7½ inches (17.8 to 19.1 cm) H

Note that only four of five toes printed in this track

Track substrate: dry dirt (creekside trail)

Habitat: mountain canyon (southwest)

7"

H

Black Bear

Other Animal Signs

Dirt Mounds, Holes, and Runways

Animals make lots of other marks in the earth in addition to tracks. Mounds that have no holes are made by mole crickets, moles, voles, and pocket gophers. See the photos on pages 58-60 for some typical holes, and also see the individual animal listings in chapter 3 for more information on their holes. Runways are just what they sound like: dirt paths that are worn by animals as they travel the same foraging routes each day or night. You will see runways of ants, mice and kangaroo rats, cottontails, shrews, and even grizzly bears, which leave twin tracks worn down over the years in the tundra vegetation.

1. This is a rodent hole, round and 4 inches (10 cm) in diameter, partially concealed under a desert shrub. It was likely made by a rock squirrel. If not in use by the original builder, it could house snakes, box turtles, or various invertebrates. (Note key case in lower right-hand of photo for scale.)

2. Well hidden under a fallen log, this bobcat den, round and 8 inches (20 cm) in diameter, is just above a creek in a mountain canyon. The position allows the cat to assess its surroundings before entering or exiting its den. It's likely used only for giving birth to and rearing kittens, or for daytime resting.

3. Dug into the embankment of an old dry creek bed in grassland habitat, this coyote den is 15 inches (38 cm) high and 10 inches (25 cm) wide; it has been in use for several years. It is about 6 feet (183 cm) deep and 2 to 3 feet (61 to 91 cm) wide inside. Partially concealed by an overhanging tree and shrubs, it still affords good views of approaching danger.

4. Kit fox mounds are fairly distinctive in the desert and grassland habitats they frequent: There are usually several complexes with a half-dozen to a dozen holes about 5 to 6 inches (13 to 15 cm) in diameter. The holes are placed away from vegetation to allow good views of danger. This colony was only partially in use; about half the holes were caved in.

Scrapings, Scratchings, Drillings, and Gnawings

During the course of foraging, marking territory, mating, and rearing young, animals deliberately make marks on the ground or in trees and shrubs. Woodpeckers and sapsuckers drill holes in trees to look for insects, get at sap, or store nuts; sapsucker holes usually are in neat rows, woodpecker holes more random. Woodpeckers also excavate holes in trees in which to build their nests; the entrance holes are neat and round, just barely bigger than the bird. Rodents, from very small to large, chew on twigs and small branches, and on bones and discarded antlers. Wild dogs scratch out with their hind feet after scent marking (when they urinate) to better distribute the scent. For more animal signs, see the photos on the following pages.

1. This is a "bunny bath"—a scraped-out hollow where a cottontail rolls around in the dirt and small pebbles, presumably to help get rid of fleas. The pellets are about ⅜ inch (1 cm) in diameter. Cottontails and jackrabbits also rest in hollows called *forms,* located beneath shrubs.

2. Mountain lions will scrape up a pile of dirt and debris and then urinate or defecate on top of it. This is a scent marker, a "signpost," in or at the edge of their territory. It's a territorial claim that says, "This is mine." Lions use the same marking spots repeatedly; females will leave a special scent on males' signposts when they are ready to mate. The leaves in this photo are sycamore.

3. If you see a drag mark like this, look closely and you'll see deer or javelina hair scraped off on the rocks. If you follow it—not advisable!—you might find where the mountain lion has eaten part of its kill then partially buried the rest for a later meal.

4. The acorn woodpecker on this tree is part of a clan that has drilled hundreds of holes in a dead sycamore tree branch, stuffing them with oak acorns (it has one in its bill) that they will use to feed the clan throughout the lean winter months.

Capturing Tracks

By far one of the most enjoyable aspects of tracking—for all ages—is capturing tracks to take home and add to a growing collection. At first it's just fun to mess up your hands and knees playing in the dirt, but after making a few casts, tracing and measuring tracks, or setting up and baiting a soot station, you'll see that you learn a great deal from all the hands-on activity that you miss while just observing from an objective distance. All ages can make casts and help with soot pads; tracing tracks with Plexiglas sheets and a dry-erase marker is for ages twelve and up, because of the dexterity needed.

Plaster Casts

Everyone should try this one. Plaster of paris is cheap and easy to find. Look at your local hardware store for a selection of quantities, from small 2-pound (1 kg) boxes to large 25-pound (11 kg) bags; we like the handy 8-pound (3.6 kg) plastic bucket for ease of transport and safe, leak-free storage. Make a kit for your daypack. Ours contains the following items:

- Five or six strips of poster board cut about ¾ inch (2 cm) wide and 12 to 20 inches (30 to 51 cm) long, rolled carefully together for storage in the plastic peanut butter jar

- A few paper clips

- A freezer-weight gallon zip-top bag containing another zip-top bag with four to five cups of plaster

■ An empty 12-ounce (360 ml) plastic peanut butter jar

■ Two or three heavy-duty plastic spoons

■ A few extra zip-top bags

■ A toothbrush

To make a cast, form one of the paper strips into a ring large enough to encompass the track with an inch (3 cm) or more to spare. Secure the paper strip with two paper clips and carefully place it around the track. Press the paper strip down, being careful not to disturb the track. Put a quantity of plaster into the empty jar (you'll have to learn the amounts by experience; about a cup does it for a small mammal track), and begin adding water and mixing vigorously with a spoon until the mixture is like pancake batter—not runny, but not so stiff that it won't pour.

Carefully pour the plaster into the track ring, but don't pour it right on the track—pour it off to the side of the track and let it flow in. Make sure it flows over the whole track and to the ring edge, preferably about ½ inch (1 cm) or more thick (the thicker it is, the stronger, but a thicker cast will take longer to cure). If you don't mix enough, just make sure the track is covered with the first batch, then mix more to fill in the edges and over the top. On really big tracks (bears), you can reinforce the cast with cross-hatched twigs pressed into the top of the wet plaster. You don't have to use the ring (sometimes you can't because of uneven ground); in this case just make the plaster mixture a little thicker—it will stop flowing as you stop adding more plaster.

Let the cast dry for at least thirty minutes, then gently pry it up and place it in an extra bag to take home. Let it dry completely—overnight is best—then gently scrub the cast clean with a toothbrush under running water. Allow it to dry again and then label the cast with permanent ink: species, location, habitat type, substrate type, and any other information you can gather, such as other nearby tracks, scat, and so forth.

Tracings

When you are surveying an area and need to record a lot of tracks, or if you just prefer less weight and fuss than mixing and pouring plaster, make a tracing kit. Have someone at your hardware store cut a 6-inch by 8-inch (15 cm by 20 cm) rectangle of thin, clear Plexiglas—about ⅛ inch (32 mm) thick. Carry it in a manila envelope with a couple of black dry-erase sharp-nib markers, an ink pen, a lead pencil, a couple of paper towels, and some paper.

When you find a track to trace, first measure it carefully: overall length and width, main pad length and width, stride, and straddle. Note these on a sheet of paper (we use acid-free paper cut to the size of our field notebook and drilled with three holes), indicating front, rear, left, right. Then place the Plexiglas over the track, resting on four small rocks; the surface should be about ¼ to ½ inch (1 cm) from the track (see photo). With the dry-erase marker, carefully trace the outline of the track (see chapter 2 for tips on measuring and tracing the correct part of a track) onto the plastic. Indicate deeper and shallower areas, if you like, using dots or hash marks.

Lift the plastic off the track, place a piece of paper over it, and hold it up to the sun to trace the track and the details onto the paper. Make notations and indicate measurements: species, direction of travel, estimated speed, age of track, habitat, substrate, and so on. File this in a tracking notebook organized by species, habitat, location, or any other variable that works for you. Use a moistened paper towel to wipe the marker off the plastic.

Soot Station

We made an effective sooted track trap (see photo) from a cardboard box turned on its side, a margarine tub for bait glued far back to the rear, a sooted aluminum baking sheet (coat it with soot by holding it—with hot pads!—over a kerosene flame, a campfire, or any other dirty flame until it has an even, fairly thick coating) duct-taped to the entrance of the box, and a sheet of clean white paper taped to the box between the sooted sheet and the bait. Place the trap out overnight where you know there to be skunk, rodent, or raccoon activity; bait with peanut butter or rolled oats.

When the animal walks over the sooted sheet to get the bait, it makes its own track prints on the white paper! It's especially fun to check in the morning for mystery guests. As with other track-preserving methods, label with as much information as you can. To keep the track from smearing, you can cover it with a sheet of laminating plastic or apply a commercial fixative, available in art supply stores.

Conservation Projects

Animal tracking can be more than fun. Organized and well-documented track counts on selected roads, trails, or marked transects can be an excellent means not only of establishing the presence of large carnivores such as wolves, bears, or mountain lions but also of recording their critical habitat and favored routes as they move around feeding and breeding (large carnivores need lots of space just to eat). The data can subsequently be used to urge land managers to preserve existing open space, purchase land for a new preserve, or establish wildlife corridors between unconnected parks or forest preserves, as well as by whole communities to plan for future growth when they write community plans.

Scout groups, hiking clubs, hunter advocacy organizations, outdoor enthusiasts, and community planning groups can organize their own track counts. To gain the expertise necessary to spearhead a track count for conservation, several people from the organization should take a class in tracking for community activists; see the appendix for names and contact information. A successful track count will be held regularly—one of the country's most successful, in southern Arizona, occurs just once a year, but more often is better to hold interest for the group. Try monthly. Transects and road and trail routes should be assigned the night before the count so that teams—each with two or three people—can get an early start. Everyone heads out in the early morning armed with data recording sheets, clear rulers and calipers, a camera, and tracing or plaster kits for capturing really good tracks after they're photographed with a ruler (see photo, p. 68). Groups return to

camp after completing their assigned routes, and the afternoon is spent collating and discussing finds. Late-afternoon routes may be run as well.

To turn your data into action on behalf of wildlife, your group should work with a local land or wildlife management agency, or a community growth-planning group (or all three). These groups can use the data to make decisions about habitat management and conservation. It takes many months or years of data collection, along with a lot of hard work, attention to detail, and persistence in the often-frustrating and convoluted public policy arena to see any rewards. But these rewards can be priceless: a legacy of land and wildlife preservation for future generations.

Appendix:
Additional Resources

Books and Periodicals

Burt, William H., and Richard P. Grossenheider. *A Field Guide to the Mammals of America North of Mexico*. Peterson Field Guides, Houghton Mifflin, 1998. The best field guide to animal identification, range, and behavior.

Halfpenny, James. *A Field Guide to Mammal Tracking in North America*. Johnson Books, 1988. Excellent for technical details of print physiology and measurements. Halfpenny also has about a half-dozen other fine books on regional tracks and scat in the western United States.

Murie, Olaus J., *Animal Tracks*, 2nd ed. Peterson Field Guides, Houghton Mifflin, 1998. The best natural history tracking book ever written, and perhaps ever to be written, by one of America's greatest naturalists.

The Smithsonian Book of North American Mammals. Smithsonian Institution Press, 1999. The most comprehensive, up-to-date resource on mammals of North America. For serious students of tracking and mammals.

dirt times. A quarterly publication of the Earth Skills school, this newsletter is worth its weight in gold for the information it provides students of tracking. It also contains information on early cultures and primitive skills. Highly recommended.

Schools and Classes

A Naturalist's World. On-site field classes with James Halfpenny and Diann Thompson. P.O. Box 989, Gardiner, MT 59030. They also maintain a useful Web site (www.tracknature.com).

Earth Skills. A nature and wilderness skills school that offers excellent beginning to advanced tracking classes in the West. Earth Skills, 1113 Cougar Court, Frazier Park, CA 93225; (661) 245-0128 (www.anamorph.com/earthskills.html).

Keeping Track. A unique organization that teaches animal tracking to communities and groups interested in animal and habitat conservation. P.O. Box 848, Richmond, VT 05477; (802) 434-7000 (www.keepingtrackinc.org).

Paul Rezendes Tracking and Photography. 3833 Bearsden Road, Royalston, MA 01368-9400; (978) 249-8810, Fax (978) 249-3907. Good Web site (www.mossbrook.com/rez).

The Tracker, Inc. Tom Brown, Jr.'s Tracking, Nature, and Wilderness Survival School. P.O. Box 173, Asbury, NJ 08802; (908) 479-4681, Fax (908) 479-6867 (members.aol.com/trackerinc).

Other Resources

We work with a southwestern organization called Sky Island Alliance that has been organizing track counts, with Keeping Track, for ten years. If you want to find out more about how they use tracking for conservation, contact Sky Island Alliance P.O,. Box 41165, Tuscon, AZ 85717; (520) 624-7080 (www.skyislandalliance.org).

The Bear Tracker's Den (www.geocities.com/Yosemite/Rapids/7076/) is the best Web site on tracking out there, with lots of tracks, natural history information, pictures, sounds, animation, links, and resources and ideas for educators.